Cambridge Primary

Hodder Cambridge Primary

Maths

Workbook

Stage 3

Josh Lury

Series editors: Mike Askew
and Paul Broadbent

HODDER
EDUCATION
AN HACHETTE UK COMPANY

Acknowledgements

With warm thanks to Jennifer Peek for her help in shaping and developing this title.

The Publisher is extremely grateful to the following schools for their comments and feedback during the development of this series:

Avalon Heights World Private School, Ajman

The Oxford School, Dubai

Al Amana Private School, Sharjah

British International School, Ajman

Wesgreen International School, Sharjah

As Seeb International School, Al Khoud.

Every effort has been made to trace all copyright holders, but if any have been inadvertently overlooked the Publishers will be pleased to make the necessary arrangements at the first opportunity.

Hachette UK's policy is to use papers that are natural, renewable and recyclable products and made from wood grown in sustainable forests. The logging and manufacturing processes are expected to conform to the environmental regulations of the country of origin.

Orders: please contact Bookpoint Ltd, 130 Milton Park, Abingdon, Oxon OX14 4SB. Telephone: (44) 01235 827720. Fax: (44) 01235 400454. Lines are open from 9.00–5.00, Monday to Saturday, with a 24 hour message answering service. You can also order through our website www.hoddereducation.com

© Josh Lury 2017

Published by Hodder Education

An Hachette UK Company

Carmelite House, 50 Victoria Embankment, London EC4Y 0DZ

Impression number   5 4 3 2 1

Year   2019 2018 2017

Cover illustration © Steve Evans

Illustrations by Alex van Houwelingen, Rose Elphick and Steve Evans

Typeset in FS Albert 15/17 by DTP Impressions

Printed in the UK

A catalogue record for this title is available from the British Library

9781471884610

Contents

Unit 1 Number and problem solving

Can you remember?

Read these numbers and then write them as figures.

a one hundred and thirty-four = ▢ ▢ ▢

b three hundred and forty-one = ▢ ▢ ▢

c four hundred and thirty-one = ▢ ▢ ▢

d four hundred and thirteen = ▢ ▢ ▢

e four hundred and three = ▢ ▢ ▢

f three hundred and forty = ▢ ▢ ▢

Counting and numbers to 1000

1 Fill in the missing numbers.

a

+ 10   + 10   + 10   + 10   + 10   + 10

20   30   ▢   ▢   ▢   ▢   ▢

b

+ 100   + 100   + 100   + 100   + 100   + 100

300   400   ▢   ▢   ▢   ▢   ▢

c

+ 5   + 5   + 5   + 5   + 5   + 5

50   55   ▢   ▢   ▢   ▢   ▢

d

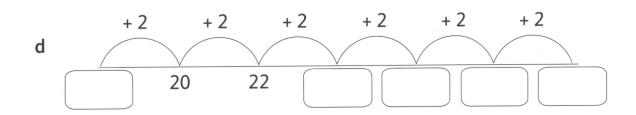

e

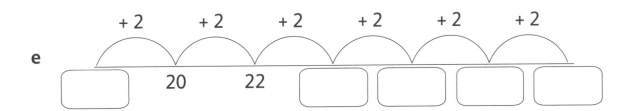

f

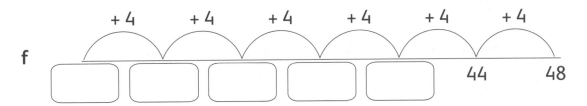

2 Fill in the missing numbers and the missing counting rules.

	Starting number							End number	Counting rule
a	100	95							−5
b	101	96	91						
c	211	206							
d	120								−3
e	220								−4
f	101				91				

5

3 Will 50 be shaded on each of these number grids? Predict first, then complete the shading pattern and see if you were right.

a

1	2	3	4	5	6	7	8	9	10
11	12	13	14	15	16	17	18	19	20
21	22	23	24	25	26	27	28	29	30
31	32	33	34	35	36	37	38	39	40
41	42	43	44	45	46	47	48	49	50

Predict: Will 50 be shaded? Yes ☐ No ☐

Check: Was 50 shaded? Yes ☐ No ☐

b

1	2	3	4	5	6	7	8	9	10
11	12	13	14	15	16	17	18	19	20
21	22	23	24	25	26	27	28	29	30
31	32	33	34	35	36	37	38	39	40
41	42	43	44	45	46	47	48	49	50

Predict: Will 50 be shaded? Yes ☐ No ☐

Check: Was 50 shaded? Yes ☐ No ☐

c

90	91	92	93	94	95	96	97	98	99
80	81	82	83	84	85	86	87	88	89
70	71	72	73	74	75	76	77	78	79
60	61	62	63	64	65	66	67	68	69
50	51	52	53	54	55	56	57	58	59

Predict: Will 50 be shaded? Yes ☐ No ☐

Check: Was 50 shaded? Yes ☐ No ☐

4   You will need a spinner. Follow these instructions.

1	2	3	4	5	6	7	8	9	10
11	12	13	14	15	16	17	18	19	20
21	22	23	24	25	26	27	28	29	30
31	32	33	34	35	36	37	38	39	40
41	42	43	44	45	46	47	48	49	50
51	52	53	54	55	56	57	58	59	60
61	62	63	64	65	66	67	68	69	70
71	72	73	74	75	76	77	78	79	80
81	82	83	84	85	86	87	88	89	90
91	92	93	94	95	96	97	98	99	100

Start on ten. Spin a spinner to see your next move.

How many moves do you predict you will need to reach, or go past, 100?

I predict _____ moves.

Shade each square you land on.

Was your prediction correct?

Yes ☐   No ☐

Play the game a few times. See if you end up shading all the squares on the board.

Key	
1	count on 10
2	count back 1
3	count on 5
4	count back 2
5	count on two jumps of 10
6	count back 3

Number and place value

 1 Write the number each arrow is pointing to.

a

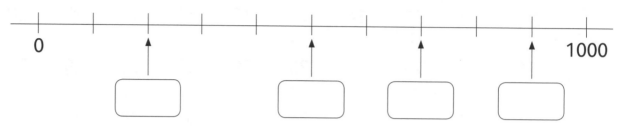

b

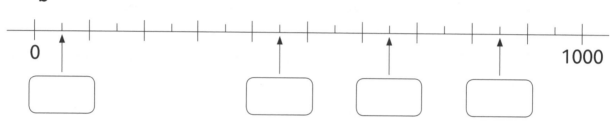

c

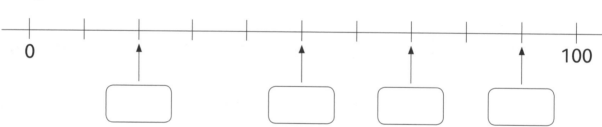

d

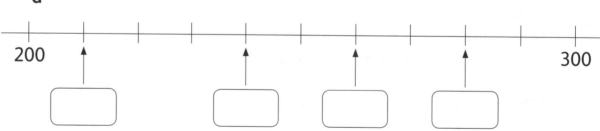

e

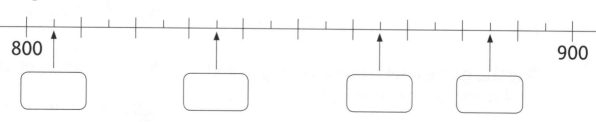

2 Fill in the missing numbers.

a 85 —+10→ [ ]   f 110 —−10→ [ ]

b 95 —+10→ [ ]   g 111 —−10→ [ ]

c 195 —+10→ [ ]   h 109 —−10→ [ ]

d [ ] —+10→ 405   i [ ] —−10→ 401

e [ ] —+10→ 905   j [ ] —−10→ 899

 3 Break down these numbers into hundreds, tens and ones.
Draw the place value partitioning as shown in **a**.

a 123 = [100] + [ ] + [3] = ▢ ═ ┊

b 132 = [100] + [ ] + [ ] =

c 213 = [ ] + [ ] + [3] =

d 203 = [ ] + [ ] + [ ] =

e 320 = [ ] + [ ] + [ ] =

Spin a spinner three times to give you a three-digit number. The first spinner gives you the hundreds, the second spinner gives you the tens and the third spinner gives you the ones.

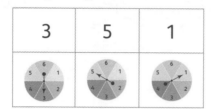

makes 351

Draw an arrow to show roughly where the number goes on these number lines. Repeat this 20 times.

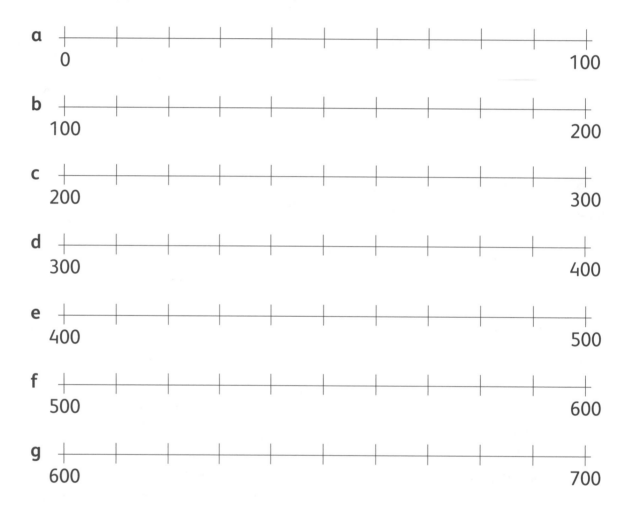

a
0   100

b
100   200

c
200   300

d
300   400

e
400   500

f
500   600

g
600   700

Which line has the most arrows?

Why do you not end up with the same number of arrows on each line?

_____

_____

_____

Mental strategies

 1 Complete these addition facts.

3 + ☐ = 20

13 + ☐ = 20

3 + 5 + ☐ = 20

2 + 6 + ☐ = 20

☐ + 6 = 20

☐ + 16 = 20

5 + 9 + ☐ = 20

4 + ☐ + 6 = 20

100 = 10 + 30 + ☐

100 = 20 + 30 + ☐

1000 = 100 + 300 + ☐

1000 = 200 + 300 + ☐

100 = 5 + 20 + ☐

100 = 5 + 30 + ☐

800 + ☐ + 100 = 1000

700 + ☐ + 100 = 1000

 2 Colour in all the multiples of two yellow and all the multiples of five blue. If a number is both, colour it half yellow and half blue.

1	2	3	4	5	6	7	8	9	10
11	12	13	14	15	16	17	18	19	20
21	22	23	24	25	26	27	28	29	30
31	32	33	34	35	36	37	38	39	40
41	42	43	44	45	46	47	48	49	50

What pattern do you notice?

3 Draw a line to join up related multiplication and division facts.

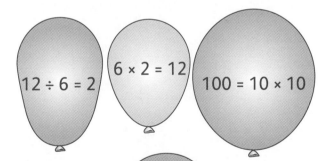
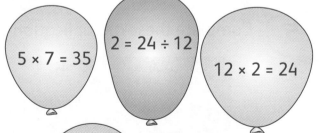
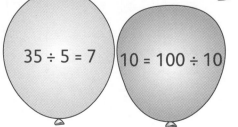

12 ÷ 6 = 2

6 × 2 = 12

100 = 10 × 10

5 × 7 = 35

2 = 24 ÷ 12

12 × 2 = 24

35 ÷ 5 = 7

10 = 100 ÷ 10

4 Use these diagrams to work out the 4× table facts.
Shade boxes to increase the array to match the multiplication.

a

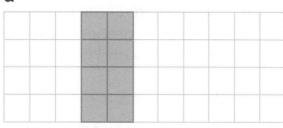

$2 \times 4 = \boxed{}$

b

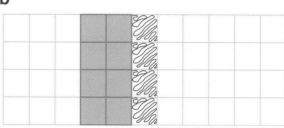

$3 \times 4 = \quad 8 + \boxed{}$

c

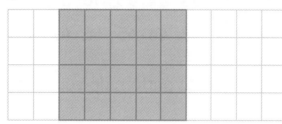

$5 \times 4 = \boxed{}$

d

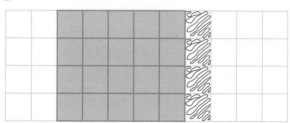

$6 \times 4 = \quad 20 + \boxed{}$

e

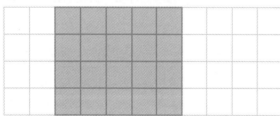

$7 \times 4 = \quad 20 + \boxed{}$

f

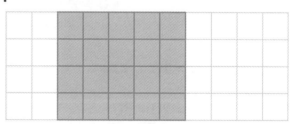

$8 \times 4 = \quad 20 + \boxed{}$

5 Complete these multiplication grids.

a

×	5	2	10
3	15		
5			
6			60

b

×	10	3	
3			6
4			8
9			

c

×	1	5	
2			6
	4	20	
			24

Self-assessment

Unit 1 Number and problem solving

😊 I understand this well.

😐 I understand this, but I need more practice.

☹️ I don't understand this.

I need more help with …

_____

_____

_____

Learning objectives	😊	😐	☹️
I can read and write numbers to 1000.			
I can count on and back in ones, tens and hundreds.			
I can count on and back in twos, threes, fours and fives and show the jumps along a number line.			
I can work out the rule for numbers going in and out of a function machine.			
I can put any three-digit number on a number line that is marked in 100s.			
I can say what each digit means in three-digit numbers.			
I can work out 10 or 100 more or less than a number.			
I can add multiples of 5 in my head and know the pairs that total 100.			
I know the 2, 3, 5 and 10× tables.			
I know some of the 4× table and can use the facts I know to help work out the others.			
I can recognise multiples of 2, 5 and 10.			

Unit 2 Geometry and problem solving

Can you remember?

Fill in the missing numbers.

a 85 —— +100 ——▶ [ ]

b 95 —— +100 ——▶ [ ]

c 195 —— +100 ——▶ [ ]

d [ ] —— +100 ——▶ 405

e [ ] —— +100 ——▶ 905

f 110 —— −100 ——▶ [ ]

g 211 —— −100 ——▶ [ ]

h 309 —— −100 ——▶ [ ]

i [ ] —— −100 ——▶ 401

j [ ] —— −100 ——▶ 899

2-D shapes

 Write the name of each shape in the box under it.

triangle | hexagon | rectangle | square | pentagon | rhombus

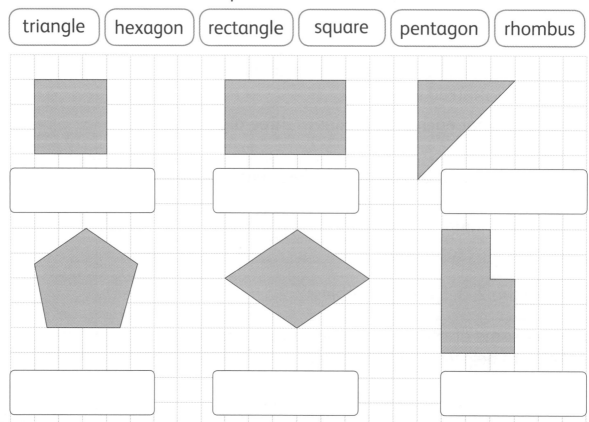

14

2 Complete these shape definitions:

a A [ ] has four right angles.

b A [ ] has three corners.

c A kite has four [ ] and four [ ].

d A hexagon has [ ] more edges than a rectangle.

e A rectangle has the same number of right angles as a [ ].

f An [ ] has the same number of edges as a spider has legs.

3 Shade the triangles below to make six different shapes.
Write the number of corners and edges for each shape.
If you know the name of the shape, write that too.
An example has been done for you.

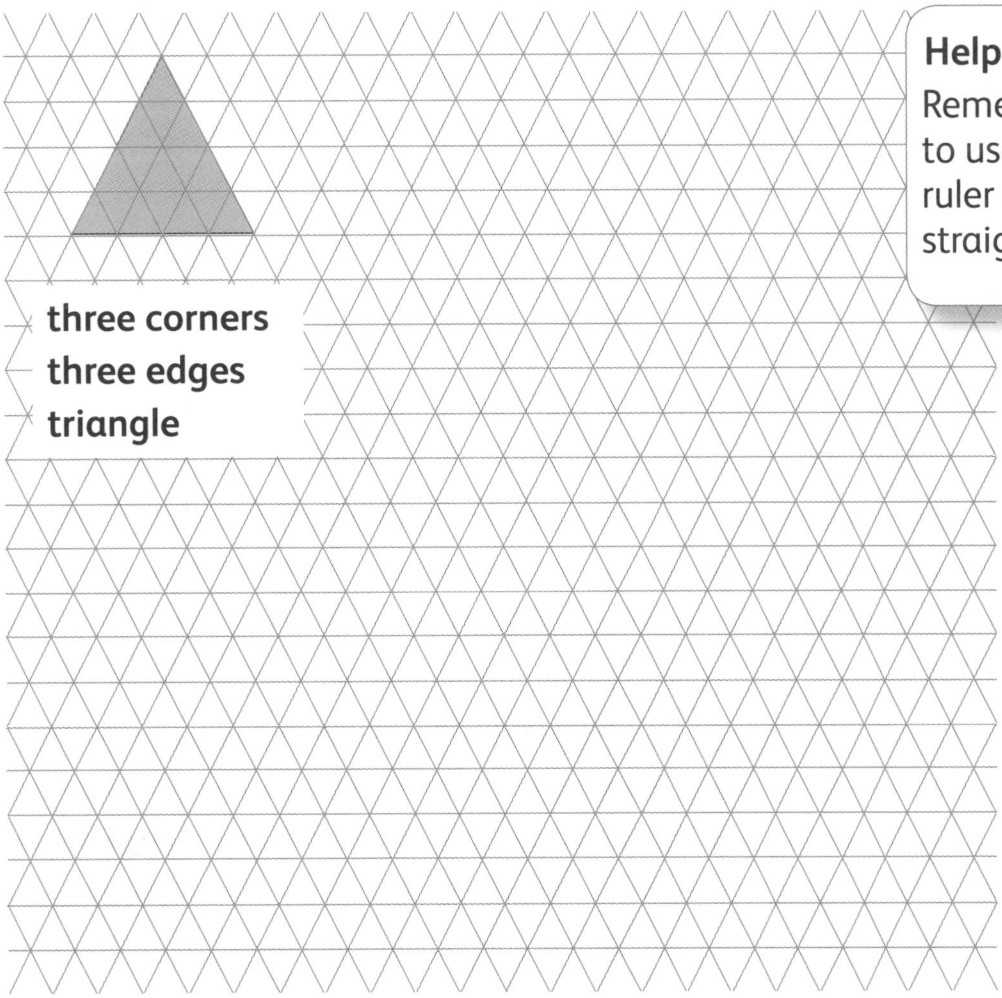

Help
Remember to use a ruler to draw straight lines.

three corners
three edges
triangle

Copy each of these designs as accurately as you can.
Write down what you notice about the shapes you are drawing.

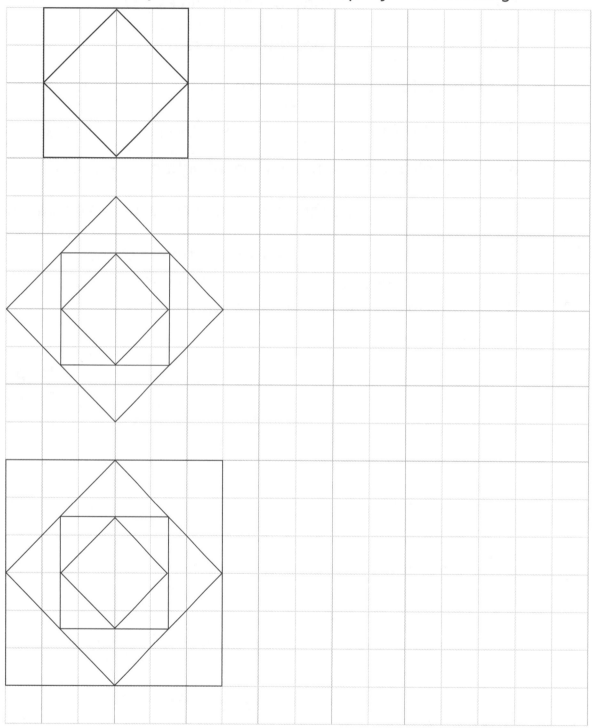

Challenge
How many triangles can you see in each diagram?

3-D shapes

 Write the name of each shape.

a

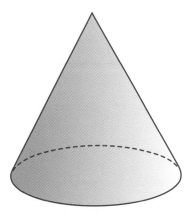

b

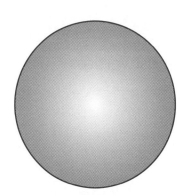

c

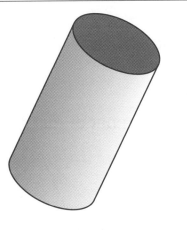

d

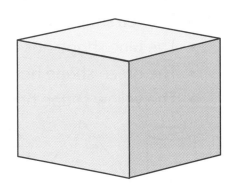

e

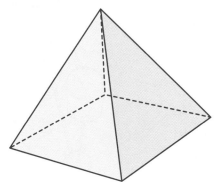

f

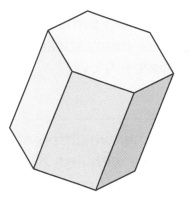

2 Sort these in order of the number of vertices they have.
Sketch each shape.

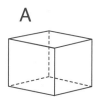 A B 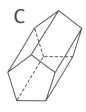 C 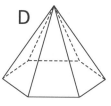 D 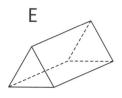 E

most vertices   fewest vertices

3 Read all the clues then colour the shapes correctly.
You will need black, red, blue, green and yellow colouring pencils.

- The black shape has faces that are all pentagons.
- The white shape has six vertices.
- The red shape is the shape with no vertices.
- The blue shape has eight edges.
- The green shape has four faces.
- The yellow shape has the greatest number of faces.

 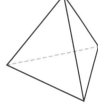 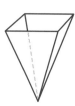 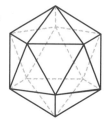 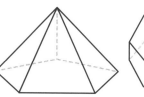 

4 Irina has 20 sweets and 20 sticks.

She uses some of them to make this shape.
How many sticks and sweets does she
have left over?

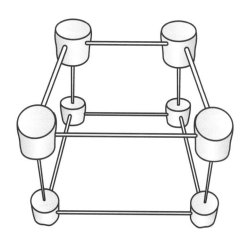

_____

Name two different shapes you could
make with just 20 sticks. You can have
some left over.

_____

_____

18

5 Draw a dot to show the right angles in each shape. Remember, some will have no right angles.

6 Complete these patterns so that they are symmetrical.

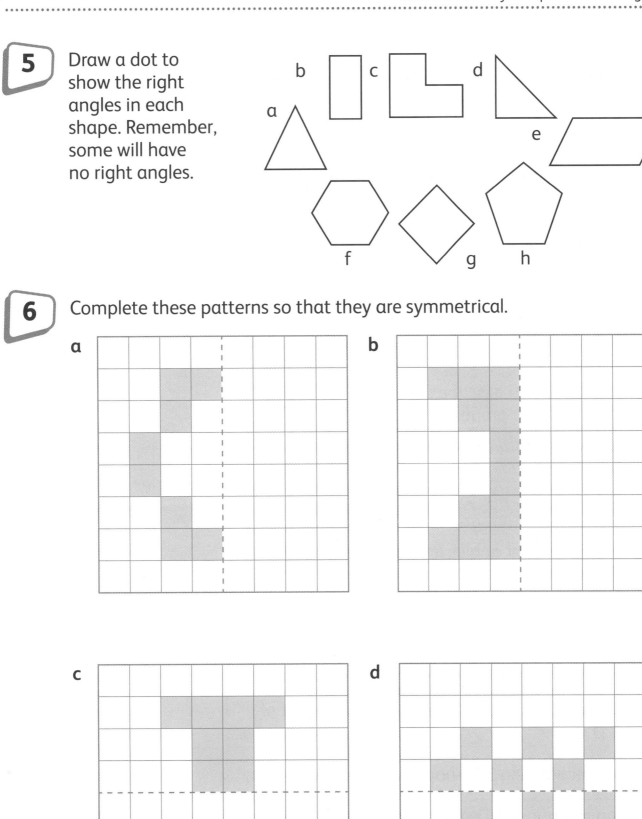

Self-assessment

Unit 2 Geometry and problem solving

😃 I understand this well.

😐 I understand this, but I need more practice.

🙁 I don't understand this.

I need more help with …

_____

_____

_____

Learning objectives	😃	😐	🙁
I can name and describe different 2-D shapes and talk about their properties.			
I can tell the difference between regular and irregular shapes.			
I can recognise whether a 2-D shape is symmetrical or not and describe how I know.			
I recognise right angles and can find them in 2-D shapes.			
I can talk about what is the same and what is different about 2-D shapes.			
I can name and describe different 3-D shapes and talk about their properties.			
I can use a construction kit to make a model of a 3-D shape.			
I can recognise a 3-D shape from a drawing of it.			
I can talk about 3-D shapes around me, inside and outside the classroom.			
I can talk about what is the same and what is different about 3-D shapes.			

Can you remember?

Fill in the missing numbers.

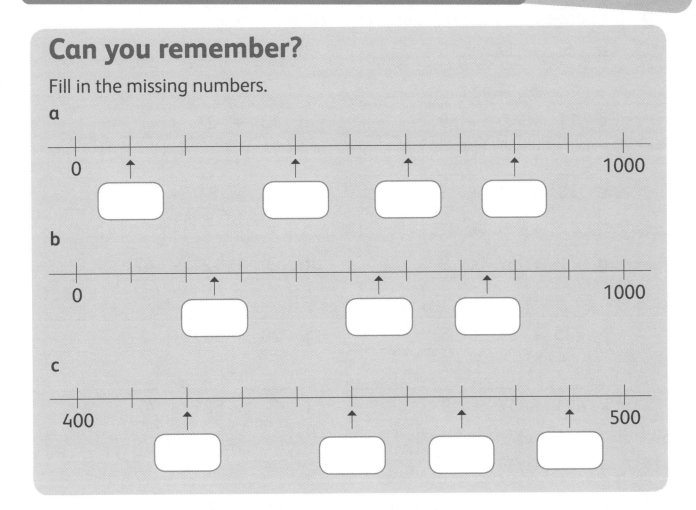

a

b

c

Addition and subtraction

 Write in the missing numbers.

a   −30
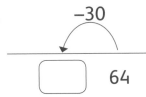

b   −30
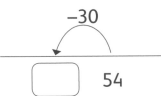

c   −30
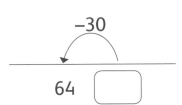

d   −30
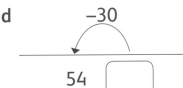

e   −40
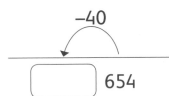

f   −50
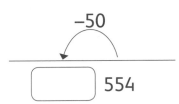

2 Change the order to make each calculation easier.

a 5 + 17 + 5

◯ + ◯ + ◯ = ◯

b 8 + 11 + 2

◯ + ◯ + ◯ = ◯

c 11 + 7 + 9

◯ + ◯ + ◯ = ◯

d 13 + 21 + 7

◯ + ◯ + ◯ = ◯

e 25 + 51 + 5

◯ + ◯ + ◯ = ◯

f 18 + 81 + 2

◯ + ◯ + ◯ = ◯

g 71 + 57 + 9

◯ + ◯ + ◯ = ◯

h 3 + 121 + 47

◯ + ◯ + ◯ = ◯

i 225 + 51 + 5

◯ + ◯ + ◯ = ◯

j 28 + 381 + 2

◯ + ◯ + ◯ = ◯

k 471 + 57 + 9

◯ + ◯ + ◯ = ◯

l 3 + 521 + 47

◯ + ◯ + ◯ = ◯

3 Correct each number sentence using only these digits.
Make each one different. You can use each digit more than once.

2◯ + ◯0 = ◯◯
2◯ + ◯0 = ◯◯
2◯ + ◯0 = ◯◯

8◯ − ◯0 = ◯◯
8◯ − ◯0 = ◯◯
8◯ − ◯0 = ◯◯

8◯ + ◯0 = ◯◯
8◯ + ◯0 = ◯◯
8◯ + ◯0 = ◯◯

◯8◯ + ◯0 = ◯◯
◯8◯ + ◯0 = ◯◯
◯8◯ + ◯0 = ◯◯

Multiplication and division

 1 Write a multiplication and a division to go with each array.

a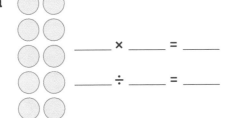
____ × ____ = ____
____ ÷ ____ = ____

b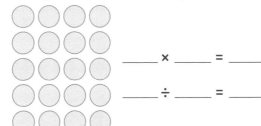
____ × ____ = ____
____ ÷ ____ = ____

c
____ × ____ = ____
____ ÷ ____ = ____

d
____ × ____ = ____
____ ÷ ____ = ____

2 Complete these.

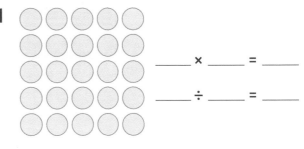

3 × 10 = ☐	40 = ☐ × 10	☐ = 13 × 10	250 = 10 × ☐
7 × 10 = ☐	80 = ☐ × 10	☐ = 23 × 10	35 × 10 = ☐
9 × 10 = ☐	100 = ☐ × 10	☐ = 93 × 10	450 = ☐ × 45

3 Use these numbers to complete the number sentences.

a Double ☐ = 10 × ☐

b ☐ × 10 = half ☐

c Double ☐ = ☐ + 1

d Double ☐ = half ☐

e 100 − ☐ = double ☐

15   20   60   40   5   13   61   3   15   100   7   60

Calculation problems

1 Write the missing information.

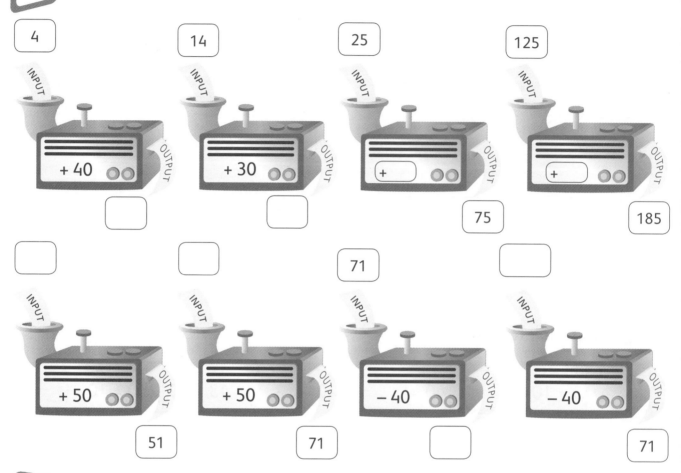

2 Write in the missing numbers to complete the puzzles.

a

3	+		=	10
+		–		
	–		=	
=		=		
9		2		

b

	+		=	17
+		–		
12	–		=	
=		=		
18		4		

c

30	+		=	90
+	⬛	−	⬛	⬛
	−		=	80
=	⬛	=		
	⬛	40		

d

	+		=	100
+	⬛	+	⬛	⬛
	+	25	=	70
=	⬛	=		
90	⬛	80		

3 Try different routes through the grid, moving one square at a time. You can move up or left, but not diagonally.

Start with a score of zero, then add the number of each square you move to.

Finish	6	5	4	3
6	4	5	6	7
7	3	3	2	1
8	2	4	1	2
9	1	5	3	Start

a What is the lowest score you can get to finish? _____

b What is the highest score? _____

c Write the number of different odd totals you can make. _____

d Write the number of different even totals you can make. _____

Self-assessment

Unit 3 Number and problem solving

☺ I understand this well.

☺ I understand this, but I need more practice.

☹ I don't understand this.

I need more help with …

_____

_____

_____

Learning objectives	☺	☺	☹
I know that the '=' sign means 'is equal to'.			
I can add three numbers together, choosing which pair of numbers to add first.			
I can check my answer using the inverse operation.			
I can double and halve numbers and know the relationship between doubling and halving.			
I can explain how the digits in a number change when I multiply it by 10.			
I can show how 3 × 4 is the same as 4 × 3 and I can use this to help solve multiplication problems.			
I can use pictures and models to help me make sense of word problems.			
I can make up a number story to go with a calculation.			
I can choose different strategies when I calculate.			
I can explain the methods I use to solve problems.			
I enjoy exploring number problems and puzzles.			

Unit 4 Measure and problem solving

Can you remember?

a 31 + 10 = ☐   b ☐ + 10 = 88   c ☐ − 30 = 123

d 32 + 20 = ☐   e ☐ + 20 = 87   f ☐ − 20 = 234

g 33 + 30 = ☐   h ☐ + 30 = 86   i ☐ − 30 = 345

Money

1 Draw **three** coins to make each total. You can use a coin more than once each time.

a 7c ☐   b 31c ☐

c 65c ☐   d 76c ☐

e 11c ☐   f 25c ☐

g 51c ☐   h 75c ☐

i 15c ☐   j $1 ☐

2 Write in the missing information.

a $1 = 25c + ☐ $1 = 26c + ☐ $1 = 36c + ☐

b ☐ − 25c = 50c   ☐ − 26c = 50c   ☐ − 36c = 50c

c $2 = 25c + ☐ $2 = 26c + ☐ $2 = 36c + ☐

d ☐ − 25c = $1   ☐ − 26c = $1   ☐ − 36c = $1

3 Here are the prices for tickets at the local cinema and theatre.

Event	Adult	Child
CINEMA	$8	$5

Event	Adult	Child
THEATRE	$11	$4

Colour in what is cheaper.

a (3 adults to the cinema) or (2 adults to the theatre)

b (3 children to the theatre) or (2 adults to the cinema)

c (2 adults to the theatre) or (3 children to the cinema)

d (5 adults to the cinema) or (4 adults to the theatre)

e (3 adults and 2 children to the cinema) or (2 adults and 2 children to the theatre)

f (2 adults and 4 children to the cinema) or (2 adults and 5 children to the theatre)

4 Write five different ways of spending $1. You can buy more than two items at a time.

_____

_____

_____

_____

_____

19c 45c 10c 51c 9c

5c 50c 11c 49c 15c

40c 21c 39c 25c 30c

33c 29c 35c 20c 41c

Measure

1 Measure each line to the nearest cm.

a = ☐ cm

b = ☐ cm

c = ☐ cm

d = ☐ cm

e = ☐ cm

f = ☐ cm

Draw a line that is twice as long as line A. Label it line X.
Draw another line that is half as long as line B. Label it line Y.

2 Convert these measures.

a 3 m = ☐ cm

b 3 km = ☐ m

c 5 m = ☐ cm

d 5 km = ☐ m

e 7 m = ☐ cm

f ☐ m = 800 cm

g ☐ km = 8 000 m

h ☐ km = 1 000 m

i ☐ m = 100 cm

j ☐ cm = 2 m

3 X marks the spot of the ant's nest. Draw three different routes for the ant to get back to the nest. Each route must be exactly 20 cm long. Use a different colour each time. Stay on the grid lines.

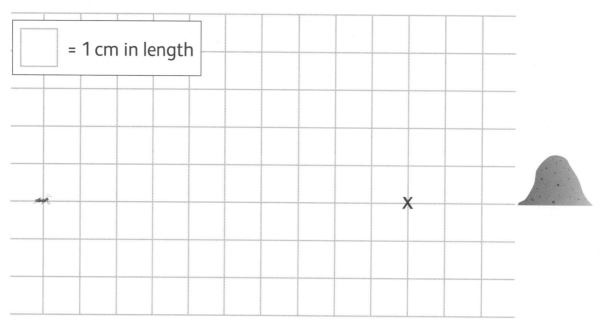

= 1 cm in length

4 Use a different colour for each route again. Remember to stay on the gridlines.

Try to find a route that is exactly:

3 cm = ☐ colour   7 cm = ☐ colour   25 cm = ☐ colour

11 cm = ☐ colour   13 cm = ☐ colour

Try to find a route that is exactly 20 cm on this grid.
What do you notice?

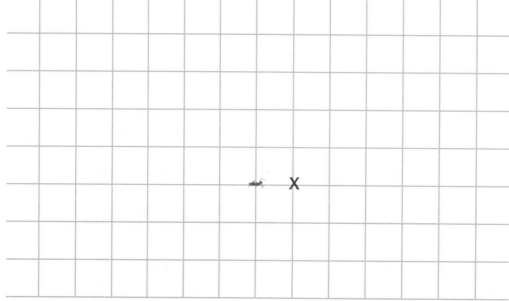

Time

 Draw the hands to show the time on each clock.

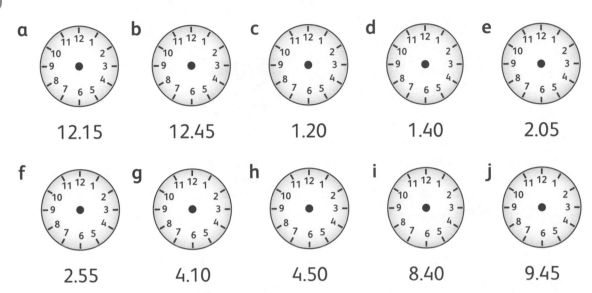

a 12.15   b 12.45   c 1.20   d 1.40   e 2.05

f 2.55   g 4.10   h 4.50   i 8.40   j 9.45

 Join pairs that are equal times. The first one has been done for you.

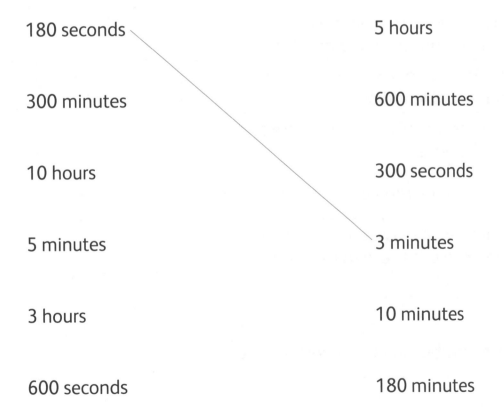

180 seconds   5 hours

300 minutes   600 minutes

10 hours   300 seconds

5 minutes   3 minutes

3 hours   10 minutes

600 seconds   180 minutes

Self-assessment

Unit 4 Measure and problem solving

	I understand this well.
	I understand this, but I need more practice.
	I don't understand this.

I need more help with …

_____

_____

_____

Learning objectives	😊	😐	🙁
I can work out the change from different amounts of money.			
I can estimate the total or the change when using money to check the amount.			
I can use a table or list to help me to be systematic when I am solving a problem.			
I can use centimetres and metres to estimate, measure and record lengths.			
I know that there are 100 cm in a metre and 1000 m in a kilometre.			
I can say what one division on a scale is worth.			
I know the difference between seconds, minutes and hours and can use these to measure time.			
I can tell the time to the nearest 5 minutes.			
I can suggest sensible units to measure time.			

Can you remember?

Write a multiplication fact for each division.

a 12 ÷ 4 = ☐ : 3 × ☐ = ☐   b 21 ÷ 7 = ☐ : 3 × ☐ = ☐

c 18 ÷ 6 = ☐ : 3 × ☐ = ☐   d 24 ÷ 8 = ☐ : 3 × ☐ = ☐

e 33 ÷ 11 = ☐ : 3 × ☐ = ☐   f 36 ÷ 12 = ☐ : 3 × ☐ = ☐

Number and place value

 1 Complete these.

5 × 10 = ☐   ☐ × 10 = 60   800 = ☐ × 10

7 × 10 = ☐   ☐ × 10 = 600   ☐ × 10 = 80

11 × 10 = ☐   ☐ × 10 = 610   880 = 10 × ☐

2 Use these cards to make five different true number sentences.
You can use a card more than once in a calculation.

Example:

0 3 2 5   × 10 =

_____

_____

_____

_____

3 Write the missing numbers.

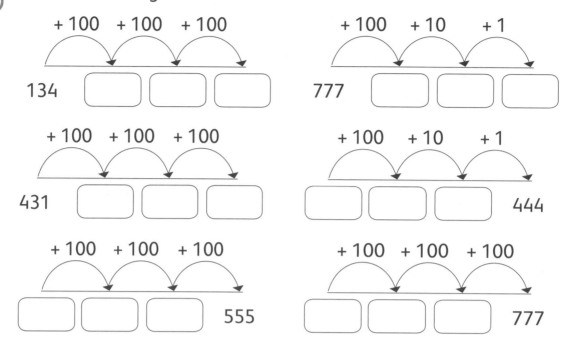

```
  + 100   + 100   + 100
134  [   ] [   ] [   ]

  + 100   + 100   + 100
431  [   ] [   ] [   ]

  + 100   + 100   + 100
[   ] [   ] [   ]  555

  + 100   + 10   + 1
777  [   ] [   ] [   ]

  + 100   + 10   + 1
[   ] [   ] [   ]  444

  + 100   + 100   + 100
[   ] [   ] [   ]  777
```

4 Spin a 1–6 spinner to get your starting number. Circle it.
Count on in fives and shade every number green.
Count on in threes and shade every number yellow.
Count on in fours and shade every number blue.

1	2	3	4	5	6	7	8	9	10
11	12	13	14	15	16	17	18	19	20
21	22	23	24	25	26	27	28	29	30
31	32	33	34	35	36	37	38	39	40
41	42	43	44	45	46	47	48	49	50
51	52	53	54	55	56	57	58	59	60
61	62	63	64	65	66	67	68	69	70
71	72	73	74	75	76	77	78	79	80
81	82	83	84	85	86	87	88	89	90
91	92	93	94	95	96	97	98	99	100

Write the numbers that were both:
● green and yellow

_____

_____

● green and blue

_____

_____

● yellow and blue

_____

_____

● all three colours

_____

_____

Comparing, ordering and rounding

 Draw an arrow to show each cloud number on the number line. Shade which ten it rounds to. The first one has been done for you.

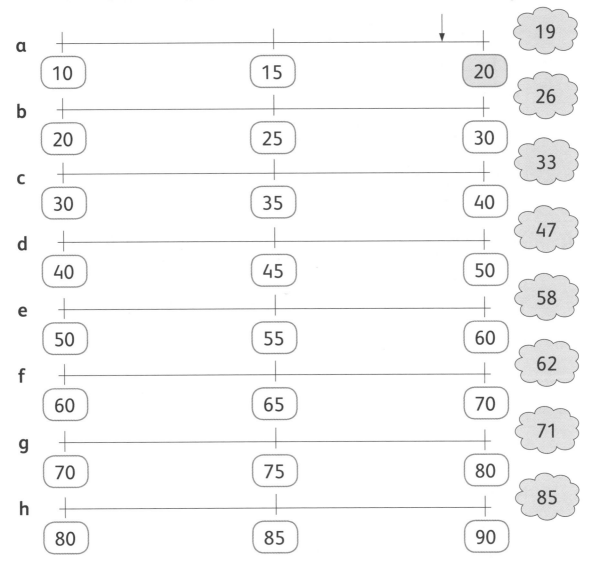

a

| 10 | 15 | 20 |

b

| 20 | 25 | 30 |

c

| 30 | 35 | 40 |

d

| 40 | 45 | 50 |

e

| 50 | 55 | 60 |

f

| 60 | 65 | 70 |

g

| 70 | 75 | 80 |

h

| 80 | 85 | 90 |

19 26 33 47 58 62 71 85

 Complete each statement using either <, > or =.

a 3 × 10 ☐ 25

b 45 ☐ 10 × 4

c 75 ☐ 8 × 10

d 45 ☐ 30 + 10

e 130 + 10 ☐ 145

f 310 + 30 ☐ 345

g 945 ☐ 910 + 30

h 160 – 60 ☐ 100

i 200 ☐ 260 – 50

j 200 ☐ 250 – 60

Write an estimate for each calculation. Work out the exact answer.
Put a tick or cross to show if the calculation is correct or incorrect.

Calculation	My estimate	✓ or X
11 + 38 = 69	10 + 40 = 50	X
22 + 28 = 50		
111 + 33 = 164		
222 + 66 = 288		
333 + 44 = 387		
444 + 88 = 532		
555 + 55 = 650		
666 + 122 = 788		

Spin a spinner, and write the score as a digit in one of the boxes.
Keep going until you have filled every digit box.
Check if each statement is true or not.
The aim is for both statements to be true at the end.

Game 1

			>			
			<			

Now try again for the different games below.
List the tactics you will use.

Game 2

		>		
		<		

Game 3

			>			
			<			

Mental strategies

 1 The total of each bar is 100. Write in the missing numbers.

a | 25 |

b | 55 |

c | 85 |

d | 80 |

e | 65 |

f | 5 |

 2 Draw an array and complete each multiplication fact.

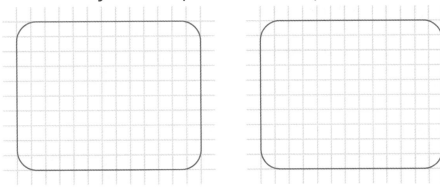

a 4 × 6 = ☐   **b** 4 × ☐ = 28

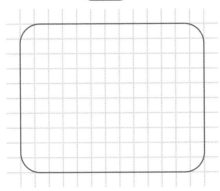   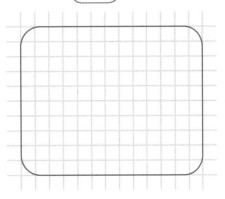

c 4 × ☐ = 36   **d** ☐ = 4 × 11

3 How many groups of stars are there in each box?

Groups of 2 stars

There are _____ groups because

_____ × _____ = _____

Groups of 3 stars

There are _____ groups because

_____ × _____ = _____

4 Use digit cards 1–5.
You can use each digit card only once.

| 1 | 2 | 3 | 4 | 5 |

See how many different two-digit numbers you can make that are:

a in both the 2× and the 3× table: _____.

b in both the 5× and the 4× table: _____.

c in both the 5× and the 3× table: _____.

5 Use a set of 0–9 digit cards to make two-digit numbers.
The challenge is to have one two-digit number in each of the:

2× table	10, 12, 14 …
3× table	12, 15, 18 …
5× table	10, 15, 20 …
10× table	10, 20, 30 …
1× table	10, 11, 12 …

How many different solutions can you find?

_____

_____

Self-assessment

Unit 6 Number and problem solving

I understand this well.

I understand this, but I need more practice.

I don't understand this.

I need more help with …

_____

_____

_____

Learning objectives			
I can count on and back in ones, tens and hundreds from three-digit numbers.			
I can count on and back in twos, threes, fours and fives to 50.			
I can describe the relationships between numbers in patterns.			
I can round two-digit numbers to the nearest 10.			
I can use the < and > signs to compare two numbers.			
I can use rounding to estimate a sum or difference.			
I can give the division fact that is linked to a multiplication fact for the 2×, 3×, 5× and 10× tables.			
I know most of the 4× table and use the facts I know to help work out the parts I do not know.			
I can add multiples of 5 in my head and know the pairs that total 100.			
I can work out doubles of multiples of 5.			

Unit 7 Measure and problem solving

Money

1 Each person started with $1. Work out the missing coins or amounts.

Amount spent	Change
25c, 25c	◯
25c, 10c	◯◯◯
50c, 25c, 10c	◯◯
50c + ◯ + ◯	30c
50c + ◯ + 5c	20c + ◯

2 Draw a line to join the calculation with the best estimate.

a	$1.99 + $2.99		$4
b	$1.49 + $1		$5
c	$5 + $2.49		$3
d	$5.99 + $5.99		$2.50
e	$5 + $9.99 + $5		$10
f	99c + 99c + 99c + 99c		$7.50
g	$2.49 + $2.49 + $4.99		$12
h	99c + 99c + 99c		$20

3 Write a word problem to go with each calculation.

a $1.49 + 99c

_____

_____

_____

b $5 – $2.50

_____

_____

_____

c 99c + 99c + 99c

_____

_____

_____

Mass

1 Mark the mass on the scale.

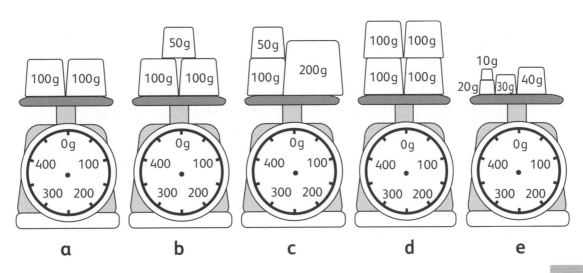

a b c d e

2 Write the missing masses.

a 500 g + ⬚ g = 1 kg

b 1 kg = 400 g + ⬚ g

c 1 kg − 300 g = ⬚ g

d 1 kg − ⬚ g = 800 g

e 100 g + ⬚ g = 1 kg

f 1 kg = 700 g + ⬚ g

g 1 kg − 600 g = ⬚ g

h 1 kg − ⬚ g = 500 g

3 Arrange all the weights so that the scales balance.

a

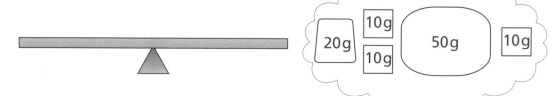

b

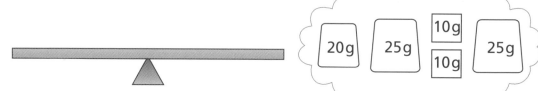

c

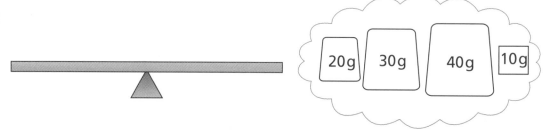

4 Think of six different objects. Arrange them from lightest to heaviest. Write the name of each object and write an estimate for its weight.

Estimate:	Estimate:	Estimate:	Estimate:	Estimate:	Estimate:

← Lightest   Heaviest →

Time

 1 Write the missing time on each number line.

a

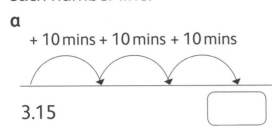
+ 10 mins + 10 mins + 10 mins

3.15

b

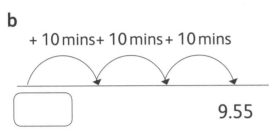
+ 10 mins + 10 mins + 10 mins

9.55

c

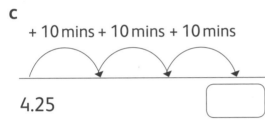
+ 10 mins + 10 mins + 10 mins

4.25

d

+ 10 mins + 10 mins + 10 mins

9.10

e

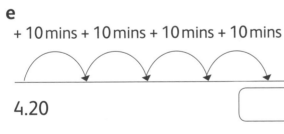
+ 10 mins + 10 mins + 10 mins + 10 mins

4.20

f

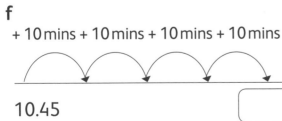
+ 10 mins + 10 mins + 10 mins + 10 mins

10.45

 2 How long from start to finish for these TV shows?

Start	Finish	Length
10.30 a.m.	11.00 a.m.	30 mins
10.30 a.m.	11.05 a.m.	
9.35 a.m.	10.00 a.m.	
9.35 a.m.	10.10 a.m.	
9.45 p.m.	10.10 p.m.	
10.10 p.m.	11.05 p.m.	
7.55 p.m.	8.50 p.m.	
7.45 p.m.	8.50 p.m.	

 3 Steps to bake a loaf of bread:
- Wash hands and work area – 5 mins
- Measure the ingredients – 5 mins
- Mix flour, yeast and water – 5 mins
- Knead the dough – 10 mins
- Leave to rise – 30 mins
- Bake – 30 mins
- Leave to cool – 10 minutes.

If you want to eat some bread at 12.30, what time do you start baking?

_____

_____

_____

Self-assessment

Unit 7 Measure and problem solving

I need more help with …

_____

_____

_____

Learning objectives	😊	😐	☹
I can work out the change from different amounts.			
I can estimate the total I should pay or change I should get and check the amount to see if it is near my estimate.			
I can make up a money problem or story to go with a calculation.			
I can use grams and kilograms to estimate, measure and record mass.			
I can read a scale to the nearest division or half-division.			
I can solve measure problems and explain the methods I used.			
I can read a calendar and work out the number of days between two dates.			
I can work out the difference between two times using minutes and hours.			

Unit 8 Number and problem solving

Can you remember?

Write the missing numbers.

a $\boxed{}$ + 300 = 1000

b 1000 = 400 + $\boxed{}$

c 1000 − $\boxed{}$ = 500

d 1000 − $\boxed{}$ = 100

e $\boxed{}$ + 50 = 1000

f 1000 = 550 + $\boxed{}$

Addition and subtraction

1 The number in the square and the number in the triangle add up to the number in the circle. Fill in the missing numbers. The first one has been done for you.

a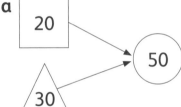

b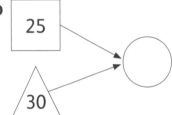

c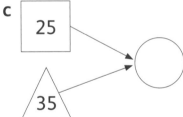

d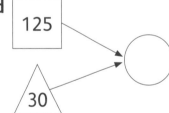

e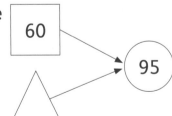

f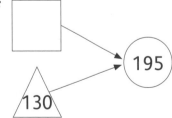

g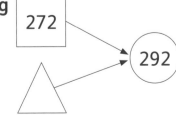

h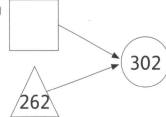

2 Complete.

a 123 + 111 = ☐

b ☐ = 222 + 321

c 123 + ☐ = 345

d 234 + 111 = ☐

e ☐ = 222 + 432

f 123 + ☐ = 678

g 345 + 111 = ☐

h ☐ = 222 + 543

3 To work out the number in a circle, add the two numbers below it.
Fill in the missing numbers.

a

10 20 30 40

b

10 11 12 13

c

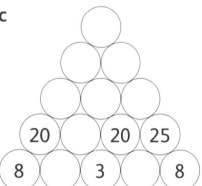

20 20 25
8 3 8

d

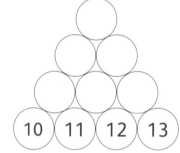

80
45 55
30 11 24

4 Rearrange these digits to total 100 in four different ways:

| 1 | 2 | 3 | 4 | 6 | 7 | 7 | 8 |

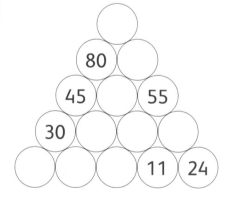

☐☐ + ☐☐ = 100   ☐☐ + ☐☐ = 100

☐☐ + ☐☐ = 100   ☐☐ + ☐☐ = 100

Multiplication and division

 1 Write the missing numbers.

$3 \times 4 = \boxed{}$

$3 \times \boxed{} = 15$

$24 \div 4 = \boxed{}$

$8 \div \boxed{} = 4$

$9 \times 4 = \boxed{}$

$6 \times \boxed{} = 30$

$24 \div 3 = \boxed{}$

$16 \div \boxed{} = 4$

$12 \times 4 = \boxed{}$

$12 \times \boxed{} = 60$

$24 \div 6 = \boxed{}$

$32 \div \boxed{} = 4$

 2 Write a division calculation to solve each of these problems.

a 18 sweets are shared equally into three bags. How many sweets are there in each bag?

$\boxed{} \div \boxed{} = \boxed{}$

b There are 32 legs in a field of sheep. How many sheep are there altogether?

$\boxed{} \div \boxed{} = \boxed{}$

c 30 people sat in groups of five to have their lunch. How many groups were there?

$\boxed{} \div \boxed{} = \boxed{}$

d Four children made $28 by selling lemonade. They shared the money equally. How much did they each get?

$\boxed{} \div \boxed{} = \boxed{}$

 3 Match each division to a remainder.

$\left(12 \div 5 \right)$ $\left(21 \div 5 \right)$ $\left(13 \div 5 \right)$ $\left(36 \div 5 \right)$ $\left(27 \div 5 \right)$ $\left(48 \div 5 \right)$

$\left(1 \right)$ $\left(2 \right)$ $\left(3 \right)$

4 Write a word problem for each calculation.

6 × 2 _____

_____

13 ÷ 6 _____

_____

Calculation problems

1 There is a pattern in each grid. Continue it.

a

2	4	6		10
12			18	20
	24			

b

102			108	110
112		116		
	124			

c

100	105	110	115	
125		135		
	155			170

d

80	84	88		96
			112	
	114		122	

2 Continue the patterns. Explain the patterns you noticed to your partner.

a

29 + 5 = ☐

39 + 5 = ☐

49 + 5 = ☐

☐ + 5 = ☐

☐ + 5 = ☐

☐ + 5 = ☐

b

12 + 11 = ☐

23 + 11 = ☐

34 + 11 = ☐

☐ + 11 = ☐

☐ + 11 = ☐

☐ + 11 = ☐

3 This grid can make 2 two-digit numbers: 12 and 17.
If you add the two numbers, you get 12 + 17 = 29.

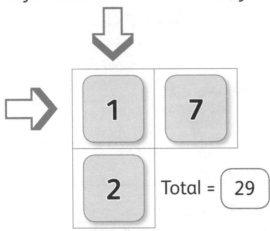

Total = 29

Fill in the grids using the digits 3, 4, 5 and 6. Make each grid have a different total.

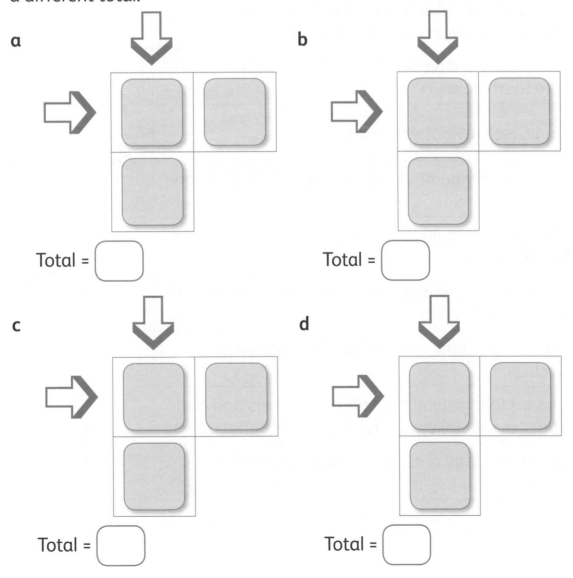

a

Total =

b

Total =

c

Total =

d

Total =

Self-assessment

Unit 8 Number and problem solving

😃	I understand this well.
😐	I understand this, but I need more practice.
🙁	I don't understand this.

I need more help with …

_____

_____

_____

Learning objectives	😃	😐	🙁
I can add and subtract two-digit numbers, using jottings to show my mental method.			
I can add two-digit and three-digit numbers when I write them down.			
I can check my answer using the inverse.			
I can multiply numbers to 10 by 2, 3, 4, 5, 6, 9 and 10.			
I can give the multiplication fact that is linked to a division fact.			
I know that there is sometimes a remainder when I divide an amount by a number.			
I look for patterns and relationships between numbers.			
I can explore general rules about numbers and find examples that follow the rules and those that do not.			
I can explain my reasoning and predict possible answers.			

Unit 9 Handling data and problem solving

Can you remember?

Write the missing numbers.

a $36 \div 9 =$ ☐

b $36 \div 6 =$ ☐

c $36 \div 4 =$ ☐

d $36 \div 3 =$ ☐

e $36 \div$ ☐ $= 3$

f $36 \div$ ☐ $= 36$

Sorting numbers and shapes

 Write two different numbers to go in each section.

	Greater than 10	Not greater than 10
Odd		
Even		

	Multiple of 5	Not a multiple of 5
Multiple of 3		
Not a multiple of 3		

 Write five different numbers for each list.

Odd numbers	Multiple of 3	Leaves a remainder of 1 when you divide it by 10	Leaves a remainder of 2 when you divide it by 5

Draw a shape to go in each section of these Venn diagrams.

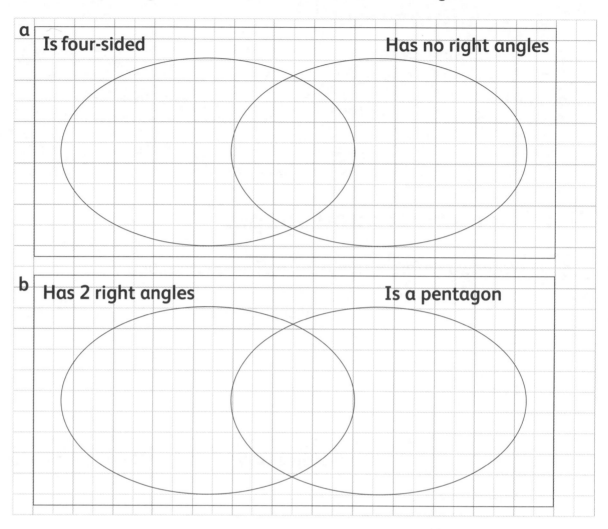

a

Is four-sided   **Has no right angles**

b

Has 2 right angles   **Is a pentagon**

4 Play this game in pairs. Each player should choose section A, B or C.
Roll two 1–6 spinners and multiply the numbers together.
Write the answer in the Venn diagram.

After adding ten numbers to the diagram, see which player has the most numbers in his or her chosen section.

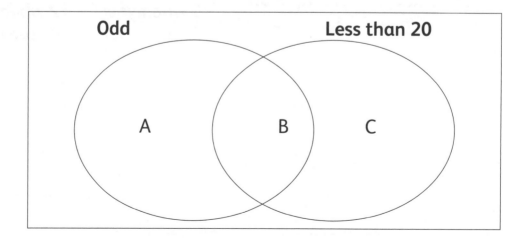

Odd   Less than 20

A   B   C

Charts, graphs and tables

1 The soccer score was 2–1. This means the players scored three goals in that match. The list below shows the scores from all the matches last weekend.

2–1	0–0	3–2	1–1	2–0
0–3	1–3	2–0	2–2	1–2
3–1	1–1	3–0	3–1	2–0

Complete the tally chart. Show how many matches had each total.

Goals scored	Number of matches
0 goals	
1 goal	
2 goals	
3 goals	
4 goals	
5 goals	

2 Some learners were asked to give their favourite colour. Here are the results.

Colour	Number of learners
Yellow	11
Blue	8
Red	15
Green	9
Pink	3
Purple	8

How many learners were there?

_____

Use the information in the table to draw a bar chart.

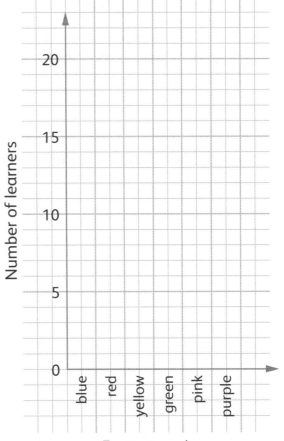

Favourite colour

53

Self-assessment

Unit 9 Handling data and problem solving

	I understand this well.
	I understand this, but I need more practice.
	I don't understand this.

I need more help with ...

_____

_____

_____

Learning objectives	😊	😐	🙁
I can sort sets of 2-D shapes in different ways on a Carroll diagram, using two criteria.			
I can name and describe different 2-D shapes and talk about their properties.			
I can collect and present data to answer questions that I want to find out about.			
I can use tallies, tables, pictograms and bar charts to answer questions.			
I can use lists and tables to help solve problems.			

Can you remember?

Here is a tally chart showing how many people visit a museum.
Fill in the total for each age group.

Age	Tally	Total
Under 10	ЦЧ ЦЧ ЦЧ ЦЧ ЦЧ ЦЧ	30
Between 10 and 20	ЦЧ ЦЧ ЦЧ ЦЧ ЦЧ	
Between 20 and 30	ЦЧ ЦЧ ЦЧ ЦЧ ЦЧ ЦЧ I	
Between 30 and 40	ЦЧ ЦЧ ЦЧ ЦЧ ЦЧ ЦЧ ЦЧ ЦЧ I	
Between 40 and 50	ЦЧ ЦЧ ЦЧ ЦЧ ЦЧ IIII	
Over 50	ЦЧ ЦЧ I	

Number and place value

1 Complete these number patterns.

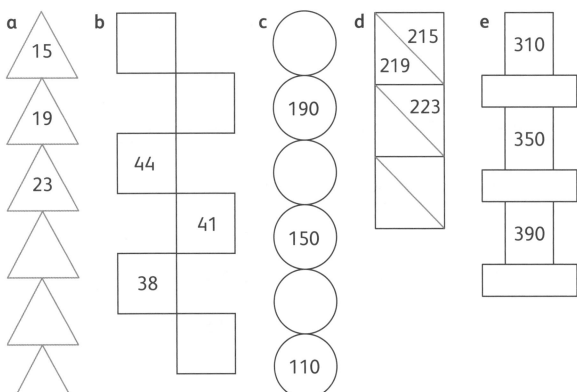

a
15
19
23

b
44
41
38

c
190
150
110

d
215
219
223

e
310
350
390

2 Put these numbers in order from smallest to largest.

a

155	515	115	151	551	511

b
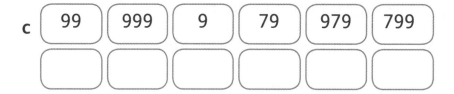

303	300	330	313	311	304

c

99	999	9	79	979	799

d
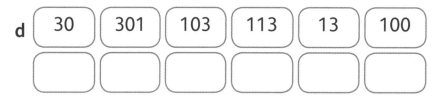

30	301	103	113	13	100

3 Round each number to the nearest 10.

a 139 ⟶ ☐   b 179 ⟶ ☐

c 299 ⟶ ☐   d 301 ⟶ ☐

e 454 ⟶ ☐   f 555 ⟶ ☐

4 Round each number to the nearest 100.

a 139 ⟶ ☐   b 179 ⟶ ☐

c 299 ⟶ ☐   d 301 ⟶ ☐

e 454 ⟶ ☐   f 555 ⟶ ☐

5 Use the clues to work out each number.

a One of my digits is a nine.
Rounded to the nearest ten, I am 40. Answer = ◯◯

b Rounded to the nearest 100, I am 500. Two of my digits are sixes.

My other digit is a four. Answer = ◯◯◯

c I am greater than 900. Rounded to the nearest 100, I am 1000.
Rounded to the nearest 10, I am 1000. One of my digits is a five.

Answer = ◯◯◯◯

Fractions

1 Shade $\frac{1}{2}$ of each shape.

a

b

c

d

2 Here are six copies of a diagram. Show six different ways to shade half.

3 Write the fractions and mixed numbers in the right place on each number line.

a ├─┼─┼─┼─┼─┼─┼─┼─┤
  0   1   2

a $\frac{1}{2}$ $1\frac{1}{2}$ $\frac{1}{4}$ $1\frac{1}{4}$

b ├─┼─┼─┼─┼─┼─┼─┼─┤
  0   1   2

b $1\frac{3}{4}$ $1\frac{1}{2}$ $\frac{3}{4}$ $\frac{1}{4}$

c ├─┼─┼─┼─┼─┼─┼─┼─┤
  2   3   4

c $2\frac{1}{2}$ $3\frac{1}{2}$ $2\frac{3}{4}$

d ├─┼─┼─┼─┼─┼─┼─┼─┤
  5   7

d $5\frac{1}{2}$ $5\frac{3}{4}$ $6\frac{3}{4}$

e ├─┼─┼─┼─┼─┼─┼─┼─┤
  9   11

e $10\frac{3}{4}$ $10\frac{1}{4}$ $9\frac{3}{4}$

4 **a** Half of this grid is shaded.
Shade half of the unshaded squares.
Now shade half of what is left.
How many squares are left blank?

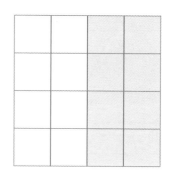

_____

b Shade half.
Then shade half of what is left.
And again.
And again.
How many blank squares are left now?

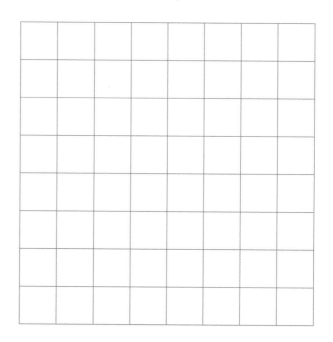

_____

Fractions of amounts

 Put a ring around the dots that make up the fraction given.
Write the answer below the image.

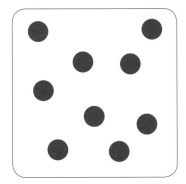

a $\frac{1}{3}$ of 9 = _____

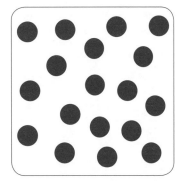

b $\frac{1}{3}$ of 18 = _____

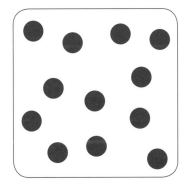

c $\frac{1}{4}$ of 12 = _____

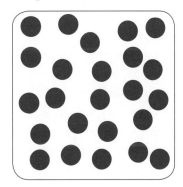

d $\frac{1}{4}$ of 24 = _____

 Draw a line between each statement and the right answer.

$\frac{1}{2}$ of 50 $\frac{1}{10}$ of 30 $\frac{1}{3}$ of 30 $\frac{1}{3}$ of 15 $\frac{1}{5}$ of 15

$\frac{1}{4}$ of 16 $\frac{1}{4}$ of 100 $\frac{1}{5}$ of 25

4	10	3	5	25

Self-assessment

Unit 11 Number and problem solving

😃	I understand this well.
😐	I understand this, but I need more practice.
☹️	I don't understand this.

I need more help with …

_____

_____

_____

Learning objectives	😃	😐	☹️
I can round two-digit numbers to the nearest 10 and three-digit numbers to the nearest 100.			
I can put a set of two-digit and three-digit numbers in order from smallest to largest.			
I know what each part of a fraction means and can write fractions to show parts of a whole.			
I can show the equivalent fractions to $\frac{1}{2}$.			
I can write whole numbers and fractions as mixed numbers.			
I can put $\frac{1}{2}, \frac{1}{4}, \frac{3}{4}$ and mixed numbers in order on a number line.			
I can recognise what fraction of a shape is shaded, and say and write it.			
I can work out fractions of shapes.			
I can work out half of any number to 40, using $\frac{1}{2}$ if it is an odd number.			
I can work out fractions of amounts.			

Unit 12 Geometry and problem solving

Can you remember?

Complete these.

a 2 × 4 = ☐   b ☐ × 4 = 40   c ☐ = 4 × 9

d 4 × 4 = ☐   e ☐ × 4 = 20   f ☐ = 8 × 4

g 6 × 4 = ☐   h ☐ × 4 = 44   i ☐ = 7 × 4

2-D shapes

 Draw two different versions of each shape, then tick the properties that match each shape.

Name	Drawing A	Drawing B	Even number of sides	Odd number of corners	Always symmetrical
square					
rectangle					
hexagon					
pentagon					
rhombus					
kite					

2 Draw a line from each property to each shape it matches.
Some properties match more than one shape.

contains a right angle

quadrilateral

regular

symmetrical

an odd number of vertices

more than two right angles

all angles the same size

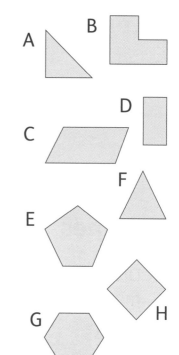

3 Complete the symmetrical shapes, then write the name of each.

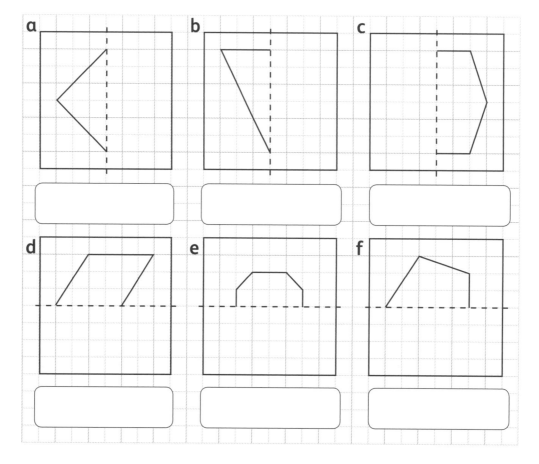

Use two different colours to design a different symmetrical pattern in each grid. Make sure each has two lines of symmetry.

Position and movement

 Use the instructions to draw the route from A to B on each grid. Look at the example and the key.

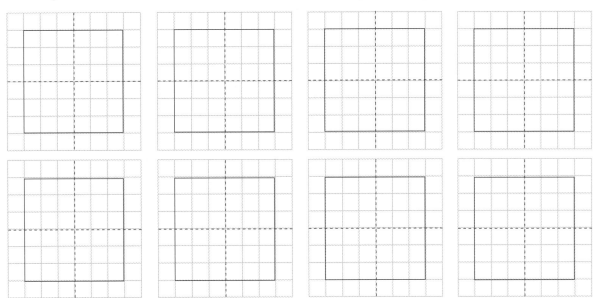

a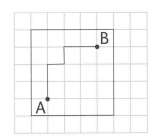

b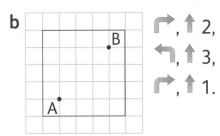

 Write directions to get from A to B by using the key above.

a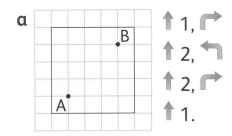

b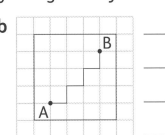

63

Tick (✓) whether each angle is bigger than (>) or smaller than (<) a right angle (∟).

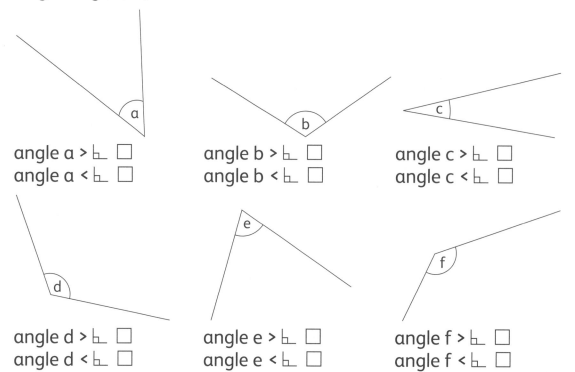

angle a > ∟ ☐
angle a < ∟ ☐

angle b > ∟ ☐
angle b < ∟ ☐

angle c > ∟ ☐
angle c < ∟ ☐

angle d > ∟ ☐
angle d < ∟ ☐

angle e > ∟ ☐
angle e < ∟ ☐

angle f > ∟ ☐
angle f < ∟ ☐

a Shade these grid references on the grid below.

> B1, B2, B3, B4, B5, B6, B7, C4, C7, D4, D7, E7, F7

8								
7								
6								
5								
4								
3								
2								
1								
	A	B	C	D	E	F	G	H

b Now create a pattern for a different letter of the alphabet in this grid. Remember to give the grid reference for every block you have shaded.

8								
7								
6								
5								
4								
3								
2								
1								
	A	B	C	D	E	F	G	H

_____

_____

_____

3-D shapes

 Write the correct mathematical name for each shape.

a		b	
	ball _____		box _____

c		d	
	cone _____		tube _____

e		f	
	rectanglar box _____		stretched triangle _____

> **Hint**
> Use construction materials to help.

 Draw a picture and write the name of a 3-D shape that has these properties.

a Three rectangular faces, two triangular faces, six vertices _____	**b** Eight vertices, all faces the same shape, 12 edges _____
c A square face, four triangular faces, five vertices, eight edges _____	**d** Eight vertices, 12 edges, six rectangular faces _____

65

Complete each drawing. List how many vertices and edges each shape has.

a

b

Vertices: _____   Vertices: _____

Edges: _____   Edges: _____

c

d

Vertices: _____   Vertices: _____

Edges: _____   Edges: _____

4 Complete each pyramid. One is drawn for you. If a pyramid has an odd number of vertices, colour it blue. If it has an even number of faces shade it in red.

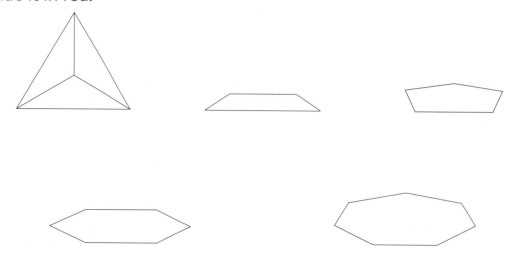

Self-assessment

Unit 12 Geometry and problem solving

😊 I understand this well.

😐 I understand this, but I need more practice.

☹️ I don't understand this.

I need more help with …

_____

_____

_____

Learning objectives	😊	😐	☹️
I can sort 2-D shapes and classify them by their sides, vertices and right angles.			
I can talk about the position of objects in relation to each other.			
I can use a set square to draw a right angle.			
I can say whether the angles of a 2-D shape are right angles or whether they are smaller or bigger.			
I can follow and give instructions to make turns, including using clockwise and anti-clockwise.			
I can find and describe the position of a picture drawn on a grid of squares.			
I can test whether an angle is equal to, bigger than or smaller than a right angle.			
I can identify right angles in shapes and use a set-square to check.			
I can recognise a 3-D shape and the 2-D faces from a drawing of it.			
I can describe different pyramids and prisms and talk about their properties.			
I can sort 3-D shapes based on vertices, faces and edges.			

Can you remember?

Fill in the missing numbers.

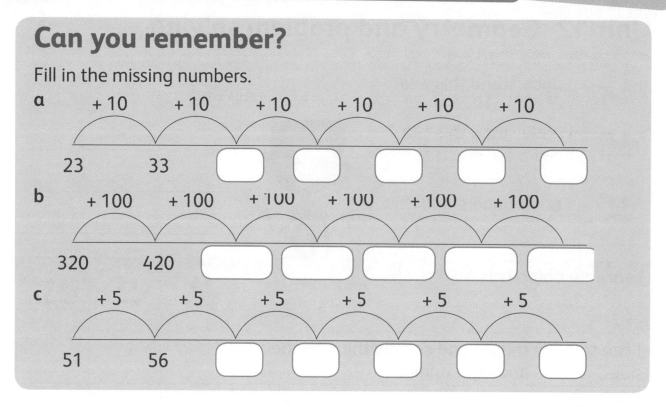

a

+ 10   + 10   + 10   + 10   + 10   + 10

23   33

b

+ 100   + 100   + 100   + 100   + 100   + 100

320   420

c

+ 5   + 5   + 5   + 5   + 5   + 5

51   56

Mental strategies

 1 Count how many squares are shaded. Double the number.
Complete the symmetrical pattern.
Check that the number sentence matches the diagram.

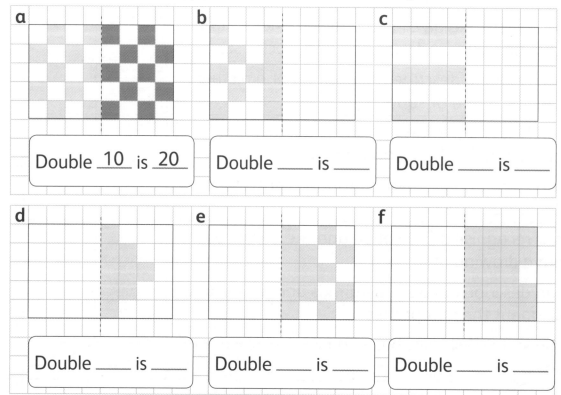

a

Double __10__ is __20__

b

Double ____ is ____

c

Double ____ is ____

d

Double ____ is ____

e

Double ____ is ____

f

Double ____ is ____

Write the missing numbers.

a Double 50 = ⬚

b Double 150 = ⬚

c Double 250 = ⬚

d Double 350 = ⬚

e Double ⬚ = 900

f Double ⬚ = 200

g Double ⬚ = 400

h Double ⬚ = 800

 Shade all the multiples of four on the 100 grid.
Then shade all the multiples of four on the multiplication grid.

1	2	3	4	5	6	7	8	9	10
11	12	13	14	15	16	17	18	19	20
21	22	23	24	25	26	27	28	29	30
31	32	33	34	35	36	37	38	39	40
41	42	43	44	45	46	47	48	49	50
51	52	53	54	55	56	57	58	59	60
61	62	63	64	65	66	67	68	69	70
71	72	73	74	75	76	77	78	79	80
81	82	83	84	85	86	87	88	89	90
91	92	93	94	95	96	97	98	99	100

1	2	3	4	5	6	7	8	9	10	11	12
2	4	6	8	10	12	14	16	18	20	22	24
3	6	9	12	15	18	21	24	27	30	33	36
4	8	12	16	20	24	28	32	36	40	44	48
5	10	15	20	25	30	35	40	45	50	55	60
6	12	18	24	30	36	42	48	54	60	66	72
7	14	21	28	35	42	47	56	63	70	77	84
8	16	24	32	40	48	54	64	72	80	88	96
9	18	27	36	45	54	61	72	81	90	99	108
10	20	30	40	50	60	70	80	90	100	110	120
11	22	33	44	55	66	77	88	99	110	121	132
12	24	36	48	60	72	84	96	108	120	132	144

Addition and subtraction

 1 Write an addition to work out the total length of each of these.
The first two are partly completed. Finish them and then do the rest.

a | 26 cm | 15 cm |

26 cm + 15 cm

26 + 10 = 36

36 + 5 = ☐

b | 26 cm | 35 cm |

26 cm + 35 cm

26 + 30 = ☐

☐ + 5 = ☐

c | 56 cm | 35 cm |

_____

_____

_____

d | 66 cm | 25 cm |

_____

_____

_____

e | 46 cm | 55 cm |

_____

_____

_____

f | 146 cm | 45 cm |

_____

_____

_____

 2 The first subtraction has been completed for you. Complete the others.

a
13 − 8 = 5
23 − 8 = ☐
33 − 8 = ☐
93 − 8 = ☐
103 − 8 = ☐
903 − 8 = ☐

b
13 − ☐ = 4
23 − ☐ = 4
33 − ☐ = 4
103 − ☐ = 4
803 − ☐ = 4
993 − ☐ = 4

c
☐ − 8 = 55
☐ − 9 = 54
☐ − 8 = 145
☐ − 9 = 144
☐ − 8 = 795
☐ − 9 = 694

Some people are on journeys. Work out how far they have left to travel.

> **Hint**
> Subtraction will solve this problem.

Person	Total distance for the journey	How far they have gone so far	Distance still to travel
A	100 km	25 km	
B	100 km	35 km	
C	101 km	35 km	
D	201 km	55 km	
E	301 km	64 km	
F	150 km	36 km	
G	150 km	45 km	
H	250 km	65 km	

 Use these digit cards to make ten different subtraction calculations.

0 2 4 6 8

☐☐ − ☐☐ = ☐☐   ☐☐ − ☐☐ = ☐☐

☐☐ − ☐☐ = ☐☐   ☐☐ − ☐☐ = ☐☐

☐☐ − ☐☐ = ☐☐   ☐☐ − ☐☐ = ☐☐

☐☐ − ☐☐ = ☐☐   ☐☐ − ☐☐ = ☐☐

☐☐ − ☐☐ = ☐☐   ☐☐ − ☐☐ = ☐☐

Multiplication and division

1 Write a division fact to go with each diagram.
The first one has been done for you.

a 12 ÷ 3 = 4

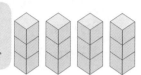
12 put into groups of 3 gives 4 groups.

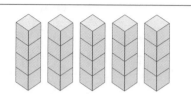

b _____

c _____

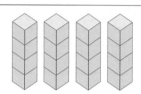

d _____

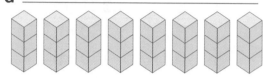

e _____

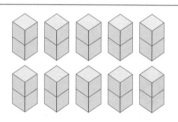

f _____

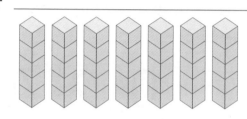

2 Complete these using the partitioning method.

a 12 × 3	b 15 × 3	c 17 × 3	d 19 × 3
10 × 3 = ☐	10 × 3 = ☐	10 × 3 = ☐	10 × 3 = ☐
2 × 3 = ☐	5 × 3 = ☐	7 × 3 = ☐	9 × 3 = ☐
12 × 3 = ☐	15 × 3 = ☐	17 × 3 = ☐	19 × 3 = ☐
e 11 × 5	**f 13 × 5**	**g 16 × 5**	**h 18 × 5**
☐ × 5 = ☐	_____	_____	_____
☐ × 5 = ☐	_____	_____	_____
11 × 5 = ☐	13 × 5 = ☐	16 × 5 = ☐	18 × 5 = ☐

3 This is a game to play with a partner. Spin a spinner.
Choose to use your score as a digit in one of these calculations.

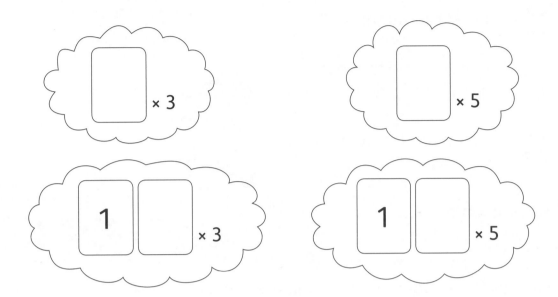

Work out the answer to the multiplication.
Shade one box on the grid that has the answer in your colour.
The winner is the first person to shade four boxes that are touching each other.

18	39	45	10	80	12
5	15	3	36	30	70
45	55	70	42	48	75
15	33	15	6	60	9
39	50	21	36	42	25
12	20	65	60	48	39

Self-assessment

Unit 13 Number and problem solving

😊 I understand this well.

😐 I understand this, but I need more practice.

☹ I don't understand this.

I need more help with …

_____

_____

_____

Learning objectives	😊	😐	☹
I can say the 4× table in order and use the facts I know to help work out others quickly.			
I can quickly work out doubles of numbers to 20 and use this to quickly work out halves of numbers.			
I can work out doubles of multiples of 50 to 500.			
I can add and subtract numbers to 10 to and from three-digit numbers.			
I can add two-digit and three-digit numbers using a written method.			
I can explore general rules about numbers and find examples that follow the rules and those that do not.			
I can multiply teens numbers by 3 and 5.			
I can give the division fact that is linked to a multiplication fact.			
I can divide two-digit numbers by a single digit number and show how I worked it out.			

Can you remember?

Shade the numbers that continue the pattern.

Predict: Will 50 be shaded?   Yes [ ]   No [ ]

1	2	3	4	5	6	7	8	9	10
11	12	13	14	15	16	17	18	19	20
21	22	23	24	25	26	27	28	29	30
31	32	33	34	35	36	37	38	39	40
41	42	43	44	45	46	47	48	49	50

Check: Was 50 shaded?   Yes [ ]   No [ ]

Money

Write the answer to each calculation in dollars and cents.

a 30c + 40c + 50c = $ [ ] . [ ] [ ] c

b 31c + 41c + 51c = $ [ ] . [ ] [ ] c

c 50c + 50c + 50c = $ [ ] . [ ] [ ] c

d 51c + 51c + 51c = $ [ ] . [ ] [ ] c

e 101c + 101c + 101c = $ [ ] . [ ] [ ] c

f 202c + 202c + 202c = $ [ ] . [ ] [ ] c

g 40c + 50c + 60c = $ [ ] . [ ] [ ] c

h 39c + 49c + 59c = $ [ ] . [ ] [ ] c

2 To work out what goes in the next block, double the amount in the block on the left. The example below shows how it works:

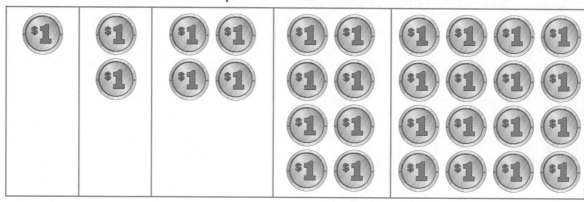

Complete these doubling patterns. Predict which pattern will have the

largest amount in the last square. My prediction is ☐.

a | 50c | | | |

b | 15c | | | | |

c | 25c | | | | |

d | 5c | | | | | | | |

e | 10c | | | | | | |

3 You can only move one square at a time. You may only move right, or down. Add up the amounts as you go. Can you find a path that gives you exactly $5?

Start	25c	50c	10c	$1	30c
20c	25c	$1	25c	5c	60c
10c	50c	20c	5c	$2	25c
50c	20c	40c	60c	35c	50c
75c	10c	5c	40c	10c	$1
40c	30c	25c	$1.50	50c	Finish

Measuring capacity

1 Draw the level of the liquid for each jug. Each line is 100 ml.

a   b   c   d

400 ml   350 ml   100 ml + 200 ml   800 ml + 150 ml

2 Fill in the missing information.

a   [   ] ml = 4 ℓ   b   [   ] ml = 5 ℓ

c   [   ] ml = $6\frac{1}{2}$ ℓ   d   8 500 ml = [   ] $\frac{1}{2}$ ℓ

e   7 500 ml = [   ][   ] ℓ   f   [   ] ml = $9\frac{1}{4}$ ℓ

3 Share the amount between the jugs, and draw the level for each.

a   200 ml   b   600 ml

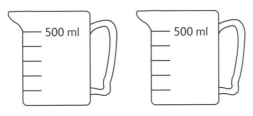

c   450 ml   d   850 ml

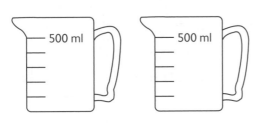
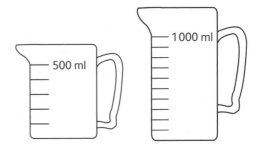

Play this game with a partner.
Each glass holds 200 ml.
Take turns to spin a spinner.

1 = 100 ml
2 = 200 ml
3 = 300 ml
4 = 400 ml
5 = 500 ml
6 = 600 ml

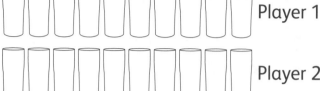

Player 1

Player 2

Shade the glasses to show each amount.
You might have to shade in more than one glass.
The person who has water left over when all the
glasses are full loses the game.

Time

Draw the hands to show the time on each clock.

a

10 minutes
after 4.30

10 minutes
before 4.30

b

5 minutes
after 5.45

5 minutes
before 5.40

c

20 minutes
after 7.40

20 minutes
before 7.40

d

20 minutes
after 7.45

30 minutes
after 7.45

Convert minutes (min) to seconds (sec).

a 1 min = ⬚ sec

b $\frac{1}{2}$ min = ⬚ sec

c 2 min = ⬚ sec

d $2\frac{1}{2}$ min = ⬚ sec

e $4\frac{1}{2}$ min = ⬚ sec

f 10 min = ⬚ sec

g $9\frac{1}{2}$ min = ⬚ sec

h 11 min = ⬚ sec

3 Use the clues to fill in the events on the correct days.
You could write the words or draw a symbol for each one.
The first has been done for you.

Sun	Mon	Tues	Weds	Thurs	Fri	Sat
		1	2	3	4	5
6	7	8 Sports Day	9	10	11	12
13	14	15	16	17	18	19
20	21	22	23	24	25	26
27	28	29	30	31		

a Sports Day is on the second Tuesday of the month.
b The Maths test is three days after Sports Day.
c The book sale is a week before the Maths test.
d The wedding is on the last Sunday of the month.
e The class party is two days before the 31st.
f The cake sale is two weeks after the book sale.
g The family party is eight days before the wedding.

Self-assessment

Unit 14 Measure and problem solving

😊 I understand this well.

😐 I understand this, but I need more practice.

☹️ I don't understand this.

I need more help with …

_____

_____

_____

Learning objectives	😊	😐	☹️
I can write money amounts using $ and c.			
I can choose strategies that help me when I add money and work out change.			
I can make up a money problem or story.			
I can use litres and millilitres to estimate, measure and record capacity.			
I know that there are 1000 millilitres in a litre.			
I can read a scale to the nearest division or half-division.			
I can tell the time to the nearest five minutes on an analogue clock and read the matching time on a digital clock.			
I can work out the difference between two times using minutes and hours.			
I can read a calendar and work out the difference in days or weeks between two dates.			